THROUGH THE WINDOW

by Eric J. Cruz

Pecan Grove Press

San Antonio, Texas

Copyright © 2002
by Eric J. Cruz

All rights reserved.

ISBN: 1-931247-08-0

Pecan Grove Press
Box AL
1 Camino Santa Maria
San Antonio, Texas 78228-8608

Ars Poetica

At 22, I feel an immense gratitude toward all the people who have enabled me to attain this milestone in my life. Without a doubt, writing is the keystone that holds my emotional, intellectual, and spiritual foundation intact. Yet, I am still new to this epiphany called poetry. I find writing poems a continuous delving into the self. Constantly, the poet must understand writing as a calling. In a sense, those who aspire to become a poet must recognize their roles as a craftsperson who not only searches for answers through an external process of writing, but also through an internal process of thinking and feeling. Poetry is life, that necessity to act rather than to merely exist within our reality. What makes poetry especially gratifying is the perpetual cycle of interaction that arises. The numerous influences in my life (my parents, my mentors, poetry itself) have demonstrated that to truly harness the potential in writing poetry, one must first be willing to think about and feel life day after day. I offer everyone this first book as a chronicle of my desire to involve my being with the world. I hope that you, the reader, find these sources of my personal insights meaningful with your understanding of the reality we share. I thank everyone who cares to step with me through the window.

—*Eric J. Cruz*
January 2002

*To my grandmother, Ernestine, for being my second mom.
To my mother, Jo Ann, for being my muse.*

Contents

The Dark Side of Earth / 7

Through the Window / 8

Floating / 9

My Artist Friend Paints a Picture / 10

The Candle Maker / 12

Following the Photographer / 14

Coffee House Gig / 16

A Poem From the West Coast / 18

The Unheard Genius / 21

911 / 23

The New World / 25

Floods Explained / 27

Inheritance / 29

Gifts Upon Your Passing / 30

Resting Place of the Monarchs / 31

The Dark Side of Earth

I peer into the canyon
sun herded to the dark side
of earth. The ground is open
in brilliant red layers
where footsteps nestle a new
break of earth

between us.
The vast   unexplained
where your hand tied into mine
a memory that dulls
over the swallow of brown
soil.

Look out with me
at a space   time forgot
to suture.   The space
            between earth and itself

            between earth and sky
hints of an afternoon
breeze down in a valley
that makes circular shadows.

Clouds, voices of dusk,
all whisper nothings.
You are beneath
every cloud
beneath every whisper
as the dust buries another
flight into the soft blue.

I wish to go down
being only one
who lets the body reach
the sunset's cradle.

Through the Window

No words in the dark. Nothing
to write but the weak smell
of your skin on mine. The weak
moonlight through the window
offering a dimmed page,
lines about losing night, you
in the dark of my room
where another sunset crushes.

We became intruders
timid with the escaped heat
when the sun lost itself
to the horizon again
the thunder of our souls striking
when whispers failed
when nothing else came.

Another glance, unbreakable
as the inward silence.
Then we went blind.
With another set of dreams,
waiting for the final slits
of sunbeams to close themselves,

we became part of the lapse.
Then I found night waiting
with a million stars
with a breeze that dared to surge
with vision so naked it wept
for the lack of day.

Through the window,
the world remained.
More alive than your shadow,
I became the other
secret of love.

Floating

As a child of dreams   I float
in a bending story
the haze of sleep spreading
beyond a thought.

Where wrists freeze for hours,
whiteness opaque for all,
the organs scream
when the soft moon throb

spills. It comes in a rush
over broken things:
an unfinished poem
a cup of wine

a trail of ash left
from the last cigarette.
Rising, it won't speak
about where it goes

to replace the quiet.
And I
hear that special flight
begin to climb into

the marrow, waving itself away
from anything touched.
It spins the air like yarn
making it almost

available to breathe. And out,
it wraps itself over that strip
of mind about to vanish.

My Artist Friend Paints a Picture

"I don't know words," she says
"that make this art."

The air is thin
with paint as she batters the brush
to make. I have never seen
paint stick so hard.
Nor have I ever seen hands mix
with color so effortlessly.

"Spaces are the parts that bother
me most," she says.

She shows me
a painting splattered with red.
The splotches are off
the tips of her brush
as they swim to the nearest edge
of white.

"You just can't make it," she says.
"It is somewhere beyond."

Sometimes, I wonder
about the canvas
about how white it all looked
before thoughts smudged
and forced her to paint
something beyond my grasp.

"And yet," she says, "I find something
here."

The red is everywhere,
an abstract piece that lives
behind her mind, walking
barefooted among other thoughts.
It is with us now—red on white
and barely audible.

The Candle Maker

In the back of his mind
he sees the finish, the end
an imagined quarrel between

what is seen and unseen. Another
hour in unshaped wax
as if time itself burns.

Where warmth lingers
where roots of shadows cling
there are few mistakes

in this surgery for light.
He sets the mass against black
eager to show an unfinished thing

aching for the white outburst
weightless in its dance of air
like the sound of breath leaving.

What he does, the night does.
He explains little to his shadow
about the great shout of darkness.

The knife's pulse
remembers his palms, a testament
of calluses branching out

moving his hands against
what is only absence. Slowly,
the shavings fall.

Then light, a new absence.
The candle oozes
what it must lose.

They remain strangers
a little while, not knowing
how to agree.

Following the Photographer
—*for Whit*

1. The Images

Being long for day, I followed
you where the photos waited:
ducks skimming a pond,
a bridge of stone you made
me pose upon, a pulse
of water through porous rock.

By your side in the seconds
between action and memory
you snapped and snapped and snapped...

2. The Capturer Hunts

Who knows moments? The Capturer.
You ran around the Tea Garden
drawn to every shadow
that might yield a body...
the warmth of another human
perhaps, maybe nothing more

than their reflection in the pond.

3. The Tempest

Your camera buzzing
for light, you covered the lens.
With the world now black and white
living black and white with clouds
of rain, you felt threatened.
The sky fell

totally. Drawn to your warmth
the rain went to the bone.

4. The Return

With images and shadows, you came
back to me. Nothing was damaged.
Not the ducks nor the pond nor the stones.
Nothing was faded.
Not the beauty of the hunt, the unseen
photos only blurred

in the rainstorm. How beautiful you looked
squinting through the rain
still trying to see.

Coffee House Gig

Now, the music is not yet
made. The plucking of these strings
makes the bones
push out my fingertips
to chip at the many tones.

The heart goes,
gallops over the silence
of sweaty hands on steel.
Converse with this mute.
Contemplate the quiet
vocal cords.

This moody riff will know
all of the people who hear
the softness of my fingers.
Enter the conversation, the sad
vibrato of the acoustic guitar
that strips skin
from the hand and says
nothing to fail
the heart.

The comfort.
It is the thickness of a latte
that warms the tongue.
When staring
into your mouths, I see
a raw tune foamy
and bubbly and sliding
down the esophagus. The tune
leaps back, becoming something
hard.

Too much to know words
that keep fingers roving. All
speak in initials about the world.
Sip your coffee as strings
slice another note into the terrible
comfort. The music does not chill
the blood. It is the period
after every letter.

A Poem From the West Coast

1. The Final Steps

She walks beside the breaking waves
California whispers tracing her wrinkles
in mists of salt.

Thoughts of the West Coast
warm as sand confirm
the gentle topple of half-formed
castles melting into sediment
with the ocean's drag.

As the curtain of dusk becomes,
the sun sinks
            splotches the sky
in purple. She alone
feels night mutter a sea breeze
over her footsteps.

There are fewer sounds
to understand, only silence
after each wave scatters.

2. The First Steps

Beneath night, she walks   thinks
of New York, her cold home
the needed walls between parents,
siblings, herself. The scream

of life, the masses savage
in their bustle to subways
those slow moans
of winter stuck to flesh
in early November.

Against gray buildings, she grew
memories fat with the familiar
smells of day:

Taxicabs with throngs of tourists
wildly noisy, their eyes
seeking the voice
that clustered millions.

3. Struggle

They could see nothing, she thinks
not earth, not sky, not the void.

The ocean shushes
clings to the shore
before bending in gravity.

4. And Yet

It is low tide, the time of stillborn
earth to stutter in moonlight
and confess what darkness it can.

More whispers on her skin,
salt crystalized like bone
sticking out. The warmth

that wanders from the moon
is a blanket, her massive
panic of breath now ebbing

from the vanished Pacific.
She sees the discarded
starfish, the algae sick
with brown.

Gradually, she hears the echo
of the water wall miles away
as if to remind her
that some things never leave.

The Unheard Genius

She sang her last note,
water tight on her body
in a midnight swim.
The many blues of her voice
painted her eyes a mask
of salt on lips
too blue, too soon, too sour
to mix moonlight with thoughts
or thoughts with songs.

The waves, not her, deaf
on the shore, on the rocks
where geniuses walk and ponder
mysteries word by word
in darkness. Under the moon,
another splash on the shore
where her voice falls
ahead of footsteps, ahead
of geniuses and words.

Not her, but the sea
beyond grasping the blue
swimmer. All night, they plunged
sang in salty air that vanished
and rose. The singing air,
now gone and her
ears filled with the sea.
Filled and hearing
the deaf walk by.

What she heard, she sang
with arms and legs
cramps and burning air
all to the heart. Her body
made the sea more
a voice than a body wet.
Her body
made the sea rise
and fall.

9 11

Taste the dirt on our tongues
the New York skyline a story
of smoke. We give the day
every name the air allows.
Amid the steel, our shadows are draped
like candle flames on the sidewalk.

Do you hear the words I am?
I hear them split me like an open casket
turning air to dust. We will stay a bit,
eaten by the soot of unfinished air.
We will stay a bit.

As the world goes
into a chase on the ashen streetway,
I take in the New York visit like a knee
on a pew. I give it every name
but diamond.

Fueled by invisible,
the twisted whines of those
I cannot know are devoured beneath
the trample. People become tricks
that breathe out,
disappearing like laughter.

Buildings.
They trip on the screaming air
before skinning Manhattan. I know
the firemen quiet in the stairways. I know
the sirens that bleed loudly. I know
about the height.

Don't speak.
Not now. The sky is broken
with smoke and collapse.
with swift flesh
dropping
like tears.

The swallowed morning, thin
with word that the sky chokes
on New York.
New York is on our hands.
New York is in our lungs.
New York is everywhere.

The New World

Dear Eric,

This letter, white as bone,
is heavy with news of the dying—
and the dead who still breathe
this war. We want a way
to forget how to read or see or feel
the future that shrinks
to fewer words.

Dear Candace,

It gets under the skin, this feeling
that everyday is another letter
signed with the blood
from towers that dropped
a winter of flesh. Disappearance
of the future and now this letter
that whispers death.

The fear bruises. At 22, I
am made by the silence each
morning pinches. I want to feel
my youth crawl into my senses
and remind the body to grieve
with the blood.
No, I cannot write the bruises away.
They must spread through my body.

I admit that I used to see myself
gray with nothing but the seizure
of memory. The plume
of doubt I now inhale
sticks to the unborn me
somewhere in the future. Why
does it burn? Thinking about it all
makes my stomach raw.

And you?
You are forgetting each face
in Manhattan already? I am sure
you are black for sleep. Over here
the air is easier to see through.
Yet, I find myself breathing a shadow
from the sunset as I write you.

Floods Explained

My child, I can't say
why the sky came
with a ton of sorrow.

Nor why it collapsed,
unable to leave itself
hidden from the drought.

Earth was not ready
to see itself twisted
among all things.

Hear the ruin.
Mud escaping like a sigh
unprepared to cover what remains:

roots stripped of soil
rivers bloated with fish
all a whimper

of everything. Underground,
the slow comfort understands
why all things must sink.

It cleanses dead things
all of the bones
all of the layers.

I can say that nothing truly sleeps.
Not the clouds, not the earth
not the blink from day to night.

And you, not yet grown,
are unable to live
with a few things buried.

And you, not yet dreaming,
cannot fly to an open sky
because clouds already touch.

Inheritance
—to Poets

Is reflection that makes
good lines reach
to the other side

no longer forgiving
secrets that flow
in the blood.

Or night, the feel of the page
words that fall as my voice
inherits your names

and gives everything
to the sleepy dawn still tucked
in twilight.

Where nothing forms
but another eye
quiet to everything

that moves beyond
a misty shape
and becomes flagrant.

Then time becomes ceaseless
days turning into a rush of air
nights into an exhaled breath

and the shiver of something
passes from wall to wall
like a slow ghost. And questions

become a body under lamplight
while all things unburied
push out from the heart.

Gifts Upon Your Passing
In Memory of Father John Rechtien

Only memories see
your wide heart lost in
the ground. And I
remain looking, looking
for a man buried.

In my hands
rest your glasses
memories of what a grave
did to your eyes:
Quiet on your back, closed
eyes leaned a crease
across your face.

Your books left in a pile
opened with red ink
drying for years. Pity
me, holy man, in the effort
to read everything with red
to understand nothing but red
ink drying on a page.

That picture of you
black and white on the bench
smiling at the world.
Now shut off
my eyes blessed with a body
to pierce—
your image is just beyond
a blur.

Resting Place of the Monarchs

When a boy, I saw the mountains
of central Mexico reddish-black
where the trees had dressed
with monarchs. Not a space
of green left among the wings
that opened and shut.
In silence,
the trees stood down the valley
and broke the stripping wind.

My eyes learned
Grandfather's lips.

"Only two years,"
he said, "of life."

The black veins on their wings
stretched from the flight
from northern snow. We felt
they came to listen to summer
whisper to the mountains
and disappear in the valley
each night.

"They come to rest.
They come down loose
in the air."

The young rest with the old.
a flutter when the sun broke
red behind the mountains.
In the air, their wings filled
with dusk, the young monarchs
pushed light. They pushed it
into the sky and let go
of day.

Down on a knee, Grandfather
sank in mountain air.
"They have come to feel
the frenzy of warmth."

I had not
noticed the night pluck all
bodies off the branches. I had
not noticed how far down a body
can skim.

　"They have come,"
he said, "to feel the earth."

Only two years left,
the young rest with the old.
They fluttered when the sun broke
red behind the mountains.
In the air, their wings filled
with dusk, the young monarchs
pushed light. They pushed it
into the sky and let go
of day.

Recent Books from Pecan Grove Press
http://library.stmarytx.edu/pgpress

Alyn, Glen. *Huckleberry Minh: a walk through dreamland*. 1999.
 ISBN: 1-877603-61-9 $15
Browne, Jenny. *Glass*. 2000.
 ISBN: 1-877603-69-4 $7
Byrne, Edward. *East of Omaha*. 1998.
 ISBN: 1-877603-44-9 $12
Cervantes, James. *Live Music*. 2001.
 ISBN: 1-931247-02-1 $7
Frost, Helen. *Why Darkness Seems So Light*. 1998.
 ISBN: 1-877603-58-9 $12
Gotera, Vince. *Dragonfly*. 1994.
 ISBN: 1-877603-25-2 $8
Hall, H. Palmer, ed. *Radio! Radio!* 2000
 ISBN: 1-877603-70-8 $7
Harper, Cynthia J. *Snow in South Texas*. 2000 (Reprint).
 ISBN: 1-877603-26-0 $7
Hoggard, James. *Medea in Taos*. 2000.
 ISBN: 1-877603-66-x $12
Kennelly, Laura. *A Certain Attitude*. 1995.
 ISBN: 1-877603-28-7 $10
Knorr, Jeff. *Standing Up to the Day*. 1999.
 ISBN: 1-877603-65-1 $12
McFarland, Ron. *The Hemingway Poems*. 2000.
 ISBN: 1-877603-74-0 $7
McVay, Gwyn. *This Natural History*. 1997.
 ISBN: 1-877603-45-7 $7
Mulkey, Rick. *Before the Age of Reason*. 1998.
 ISBN: 1-877603-60-0 $10
Peckham, Joel B. *Nightwalking*. 2001.
 ISBN: 1-877603-73-2 $12
Radasci, Geri. *Ancient Music*. 2000.
 ISBN: 1-877603-67-8 $7
Reposa, Carol Coffee. *The Green Room*. 1999.
 ISBN: 1-877603-59-7 $7
Rodriguez, Michael. *Humidity Moon*. 1998.
 ISBN: 1-877603-54-6 $15
Scrimgeour, J. D. *Spin Moves*. 2001.
 ISBN: 1-877603-71-6 $8
Seale, Jan Epron. *The Yin of It*, 2000.
 ISBN: 1-877603-68-6 $6
Teichmann, Sandra Gail. *Slow Mud*. 1998.
 ISBN: 1-877603-55-4 $10
Treviño-Benavides, Frances. *Mama & Other Tragedies*. 1999.
 ISBN: 1-877603-63-5 $8
Van Cleave, Ryan G. *Say Hello*. 2001.
 ISBN: 1-877603-72-4 $12
Van Riper, Craig. *Convenient Danger*. 2000.
 ISBN: 1-877603-62-7 $7